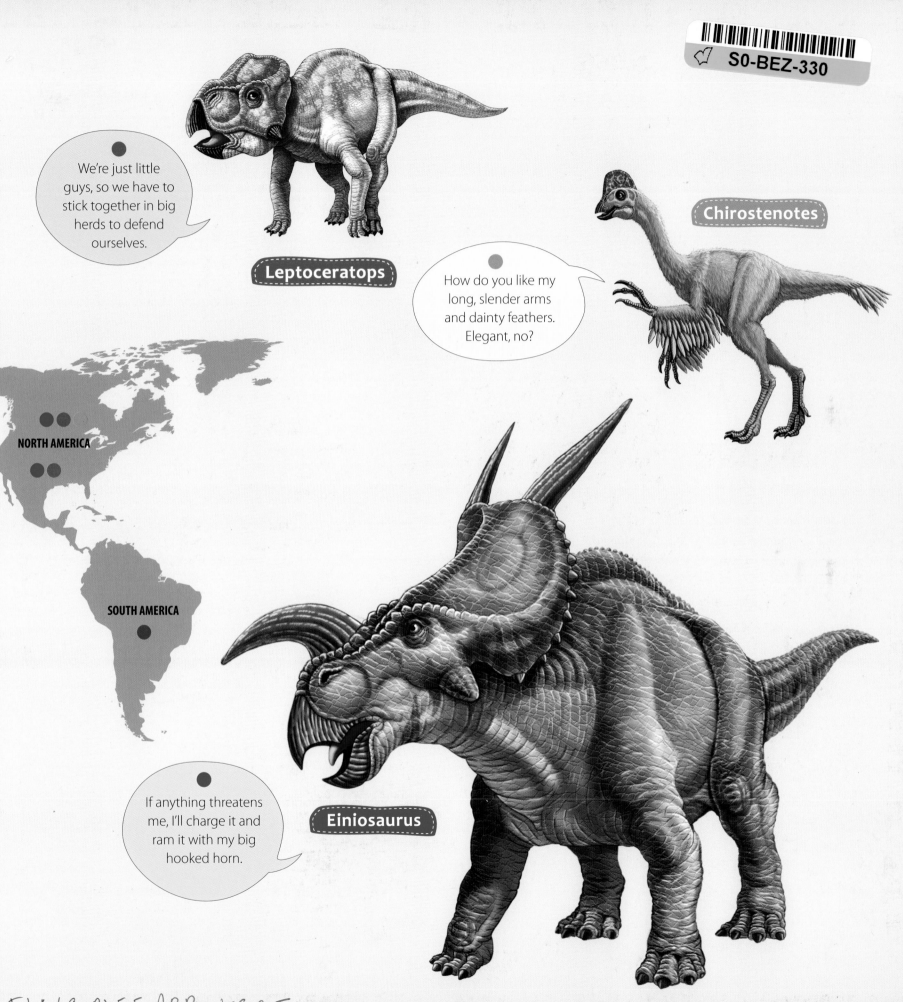

big & SMALL

Original Korean text and illustrations by Dreaming Tortoise
Korean edition © Aram Publishing

This English edition published by big & SMALL in 2017
by arrangement with Aram Publishing
English text edited by Scott Forbes
English edition © big & SMALL 2017

Distributed in the United States and Canada by
Lerner Publishing Group, Inc.
241 First Avenue North
Minneapolis, MN 55401 U.S.A.
www.lernerbooks.com

Photo credits:
Page 29, center: © FunkMonk; bottom: © FunkMonk

ISBN: 978-1-925235-21-0
Printed in Korea

To learn more about dinosaur fossils, see page 28.
For information on the main groups of dinosaurs,
see the Dinosaur Family Tree on page 30.

Hook-nosed
Einiosaurus

Einiosaurus

big & SMALL

Pelecanimimus

SAY IT:
Peh-leh-ca-ni-MY-mus

A group of Pelecanimimus had found a swamp full of giant dragonfly-like insects called Meganeura. They were leaping around trying to catch the insects as they flew past. Every so often, there was a snap and a crunch as one of the Pelecanimimus caught and ate an insect.

Pelecanimimus had a pouch in its throat, a bit like that of a pelican. In fact, its name means "pelican mimic." Pelicanimimus could store food in this pouch for eating later. It had more than 220 teeth in its jaws, so it could chew through the toughest leaves and crunch up small bones.

7

The Pelecanimimus were so busy trying to catch the Meganeuras that they didn't notice a fearsome meat-eater, Neovenator, approaching. Then it let out a roar. The Pelecanimimus saw it and sped off.

With their long, powerful legs, the Pelecanimimus could run faster than almost any other dinosaur. The Neovenator could not keep up, and soon gave up the chase.

HEIGHT: 3.3 feet (1 meter)

LENGTH: 6.6–8 feet (2–2.5 meters)

WEIGHT: 55–100 tons (25–40 kilograms)

WHEN IT LIVED: TRIASSIC   JURASSIC   CRETACEOUS

GROUP: Theropods   DIET: Meat

WHERE IT LIVED: Europe (western Europe)

8

NEOVENATOR

GROUP: Theropods
DIET: Meat
WHEN IT LIVED: Early Cretaceous
WHERE IT LIVED: Western Europe
(England)
LENGTH: 26 feet (8 meters)
HEIGHT: 8 feet (2.5 meters)
WEIGHT: 1650 pounds
(750 kilograms)

Dilong

SAY IT:
Dee-long

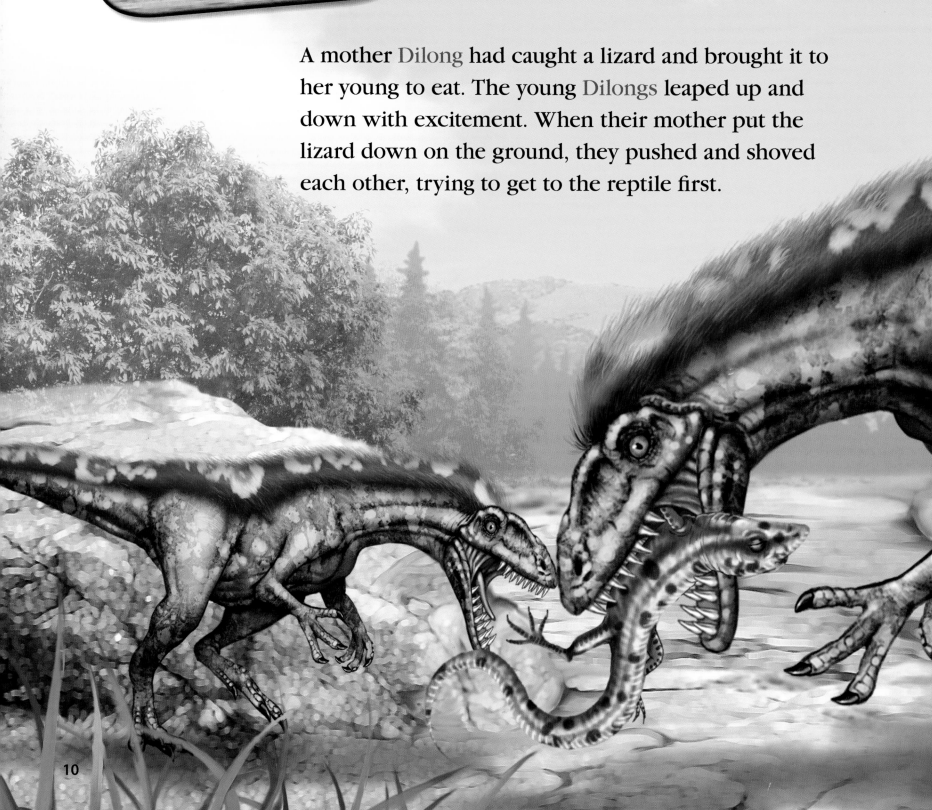

A mother Dilong had caught a lizard and brought it to her young to eat. The young Dilongs leaped up and down with excitement. When their mother put the lizard down on the ground, they pushed and shoved each other, trying to get to the reptile first.

The name Dilong means "emperor dragon."
It was given this name because it was related to
Tyrannosaurus, the so-called king of the dinosaurs.
Dilong shared some features with Tyrannosaurus,
including big jaws with long, sharp teeth.
However, it was much smaller than Tyrannosaurus.

Dilong's head, neck, and back were covered in a layer of short feathers. This helped keep it warm.

LENGTH: 6.6 feet
(2 meters)

HEIGHT: 2.6 feet
(0.8 meters)

WEIGHT: 22 pounds
(10 kilograms)

WHEN IT LIVED: TRIASSIC   JURASSIC   CRETACEOUS

GROUP: Theropods

DIET: Meat

WHERE IT LIVED:
Asia (China)

As they grew bigger, the young Dilongs began to hunt by themselves. One morning they spotted a Psittacosaurus. They ran up on either side of it. Then, as one of the Dilongs leaped onto its back, grabbing hold with its sharp claws, the others attacked it from the sides, biting at its legs and flanks.

Soon the Dilongs had brought the Psittacosaurus to the ground and killed it. It would be the first large meal they had caught by themselves. Their mother would be pleased!

PSITTACOSAURUS

GROUP: Ceratopsians
DIET: Plants
WHEN IT LIVED: Early Cretaceous
WHERE IT LIVED: Asia (China, Mongolia)
LENGTH: 3.3–6.6 feet (1–2 meters)
HEIGHT: 4.3 feet (1.3 meters)
WEIGHT: 55 pounds
(25 kilograms)

13

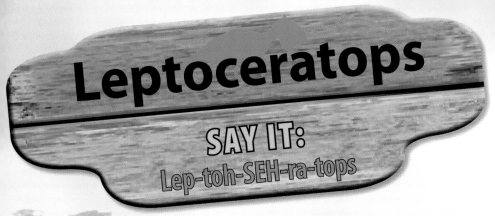

Leptoceratops

SAY IT:
Lep-toh-SEH-ra-tops

A Leptoceratops and its baby were feeding in a forest. When the mother spotted a Dromeosaurus coming toward them, she knew they had to get away. She urged her baby to run as fast as it could. The baby was scared, but the mother steered it into dense bushes where she knew the Dromeosaurus could not follow. There they were safe — for the time being, at least.

DROMEOSAURUS

GROUP: Theropods
DIET: Meat
WHEN IT LIVED: Late Cretaceous
WHERE IT LIVED: North America
(USA, Canada)
LENGTH: 6 feet (1.8 meters)
HEIGHT: 4.3 feet (1.3 meters)
WEIGHT: 33–77 pounds
(15–35 kilograms)

LENGTH: 8 feet
(2.5 meters)
HEIGHT: 4 feet
(1.2 meters)
WEIGHT: 265 pounds
(120 kilograms)

WHEN IT LIVED: TRIASSIC | JURASSIC | CRETACEOUS

GROUP: Ceratopsians
DIET: Plants

WHERE IT LIVED:
North America
(USA, Canada)

15

Carcharodontosaurus

SAY IT:
Car-ka-ro-don-toh-SAW-rus

A Carcharodontosaurus was getting frustrated. It had been chasing an Ouranosaurus all morning without managing to catch it. Even though Carcharodontosaurus was the biggest meat-eater around, it wasn't always successful at catching prey. So it headed off in a different direction to see what it could find.

OURANOSAURUS

GROUP: Ornithopods
DIET: Plants
WHEN IT LIVED: Early Cretaceous
WHERE IT LIVED: Africa (Niger)
LENGTH: 20 feet (6 meters)
HEIGHT: 6.6 feet (2 meters)
WEIGHT: 1.1 tons
(1 tonne)

Carcharodontosaurus means "shark-tooth reptile." It was given that name because it had big, curved teeth like those of a shark. These teeth had jagged edges like a saw, which helped them cut through flesh and bone.

Scientists have worked out that Carcharodontosaurus was related to other large meat-eaters on other continents, including Giganotosaurus in South America and Acrocanthosaurus in North America.

HEIGHT: **20 feet** (6 meters)

LENGTH: **40–46 feet** (12–14 meters)

WEIGHT: **6.6–8.3 tons** (6–7.5 tonnes)

WHEN IT LIVED: TRIASSIC | JURASSIC | CRETACEOUS

GROUP: **Theropods**

DIET: **Plants**

WHERE IT LIVED: **Africa** (Algeria, Morocco, Niger)

The Carcharodontosaurus then came across two Paralititans. These were huge, long-necked plant-eaters that used their long tails to whack attackers. They would be too hard for the Carcharodontosaurus to attack alone. But at that moment another Carcharodontosaurus arrived. Working together, they might just grab themselves a huge, tasty meal!

Carcharodontosaurus was even bigger than Tyrannosaurus, although its bite wasn't as strong.

PARALITITAN

GROUP: Sauropods
DIET: Plants
WHEN IT LIVED: Early Cretaceous
WHERE IT LIVED: Africa
(Egypt, Morocco)
LENGTH: 88–100 feet (27–30 meters)
HEIGHT: 30 feet (9 meters)
WEIGHT: 66 tons
(60 tonnes)

19

Chirostenotes

The Chirostenotes were hunting among some large rocks. One of them caught a lizard, but there seemed to be little else to eat there. So the others decided to explore a different area.

Chirostenotes was a small bird-like dinosaur, with long legs and a crest, and feathers all over its body. Its name means "narrow-handed," and it had long slender arms and hands. At the end of its middle finger was a long, hooked claw that was useful for stabbing prey and digging into insect nests.

LENGTH: 6.6 feet
(2 meters)

HEIGHT: 4.3 feet
(1.3 meters)

WEIGHT: 55 pounds
(25 kilograms)

WHEN IT LIVED:	TRIASSIC	JURASSIC	CRETACEOUS

GROUP: Theropods	DIET: Meat and plants

WHERE IT LIVED:
North America
(Canada)

Soon the two Chirostenotes came across a Pachycephalosaurus nest. Only two young male Pachycephalosaurus were there, and they were too busy play-fighting with each other to notice what was going on around them. The Chirostenotes sneaked up to the nest and began eating some of the eggs there.

PACHYCEPHALOSAURUS

GROUP: Pachycephalosaurs
DIET: Plants
WHEN IT LIVED: Late Cretaceous
WHERE IT LIVED: North America (Canada),
Asia (South Korea)
LENGTH: 13–16 feet (4–5 meters)
HEIGHT: 6.6 feet (2 meters)
WEIGHT: 440–66 pounds
(250–300 kilograms)

Chirostenotes used the long feathers on its arms to waft insects toward its mouth. It had a tough beak but it didn't have any teeth, so it could only eat smaller tidbits, such as lizards, small mammals, and insects, as well as fruit, seeds, and eggs.

Einiosaurus

A herd of Einiosaurus were marching across the plains, alongside a group of giant Alamosaurus. A young Einiosaurus was getting tired, but its mother urged it to keep going. They needed to find a fresh supply of food soon.

24

ALAMOSAURUS

GROUP: Sauropods
DIET: Plants
WHEN IT LIVED: Late Cretaceous
WHERE IT LIVED: North America
(USA)
LENGTH: 66 feet (20 meters)
HEIGHT: 20 feet (6 meters)
WEIGHT: 33 tons
(30 tonnes)

Einiosaurus means "buffalo lizard," and this broad, heavy dinosaur really did look like a buffalo, with its large head and horns. The long horns and its big neck frill made Einiosaurus seem scary. But that was just to frighten off would-be attackers. Really, it was a gentle creature and ate only plants.

Two of the Einiosaurus spotted a dangerous Daspletosaurus approaching. They warned the rest of the herd, then turned to face the vicious meat-eater.

LENGTH: **23 feet**
(7 meters)

HEIGHT: **6.6 feet**
(2 meters)

WEIGHT: **5.5 tons**
(5 tonnes)

WHEN IT LIVED:	TRIASSIC	JURASSIC	CRETACEOUS

GROUP: **Ceratopsians**	DIET: **Plants**

WHERE IT LIVED:
North America
(USA, Canada)

The horn on Einiosaurus' snout curved downward, so it wasn't ideal for stabbing attackers. But Einiosaurus could still use it to ram and break the legs of large dinsoars.

DASPLETOSAURUS

GROUP: Theropods
DIET: Meat
WHEN IT LIVED: Late Cretaceous
WHERE IT LIVED: North America (Canada)
LENGTH: 30 feet (9 meters)
HEIGHT: 16 feet (5 meters)
WEIGHT: 2.2 tons
(2 tonnes)

Einiosaurus' strong beak-like mouth had a sharp edge that was good for ripping up plants. It also had lots of teeth for chewing the plant pieces into a mush.

Dinosaur Fossils

Fossils are the remains of dinosaurs. They can be hard parts of dinosaurs, such as bones and teeth, that have slowly turned to stone. Or they may be impressions of bones, teeth, or skin preserved in rocks.

▶ Pelecanimimus

Pelecanimimus

The first Pelecanimimus fossil was found in Spain in July 1993. It was very well preserved and included most of the body apart from the back legs and tail. The dinosaur's crest and neck pouch were clearly visible, as well as what appeared to be strands of hair. However, scientists later decided these strands were really skin patterns and the imprints of veins under the skin.

Dilong

Four Dilong fossils were found together in the province of Liaoning in China. These indicated that this dinosaur had feathers. These were not feathers for flying, however, but just to keep the dinosaur warm. After studying the fossils carefully, scientists decided that this dinosaur was an early relative of Tyrannosaurus. In 2004, the Chinese dinosaur expert Xu Xing gave it the name Dilong, meaning "emperor dragon."

◀ Dilong

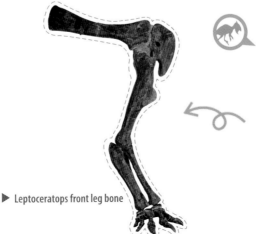

▶ Leptoceratops front leg bone

Leptoceratops

Famous dinosaur hunter Barnum Brown discovered the first Leptoceratops fossil, in the Red Deer Valley, in Alberta, Canada, in 1910. He described and named the dinosaur four years later. The first fossil was missing part of the skull, however, and it wasn't until 1947 that a complete skeleton was found, by Charles Mortram Sternberg.

▲ Carcharodontosaurus skull fossil

Carcharodontosaurus

When the first Carcharodontosaurus fossils were found in Algeria, North Africa, in 1921, scientists decided they belonged to a dinosaur called Megalosaurus. However, a few years later, German expert Ernst Stromer worked out that the fossils were from a previously unknown species, and it was given the name Carcharodontosaurus in 1931. In 1995, US dinosaur hunter Paul Sereno found a complete Carcharodontosaurus skull close to where the first fossils had been found in Algeria.

Chirostenotes

In 1914, George Fryer Sternberg discovered the first Chirostenotes fossils — a pair of hands — in Alberta, Canada. A Canadian dinosaur expert, Lawrence Lambe, then studied the fossils but died before completing his work, and it was not until 1924 that the dinosaur was named, by Charles Gilmore. Later discoveries of further fossils helped paint a clearer picture of this dinosaur.

◄ Model of a Chirostenotes skeleton

▶ Model of an Einiosaurus skull

Einiosaurus

All the fossils of Einiosaurus found so far come from the same site in Montana, USA. The first were discovered in 1985 by the famous American dinosaur hunter Jack Horner, and many more have been dug up since then. The dinosaur's name comes partly from a Blackfeet Indian word *eini*, meaning "buffalo."

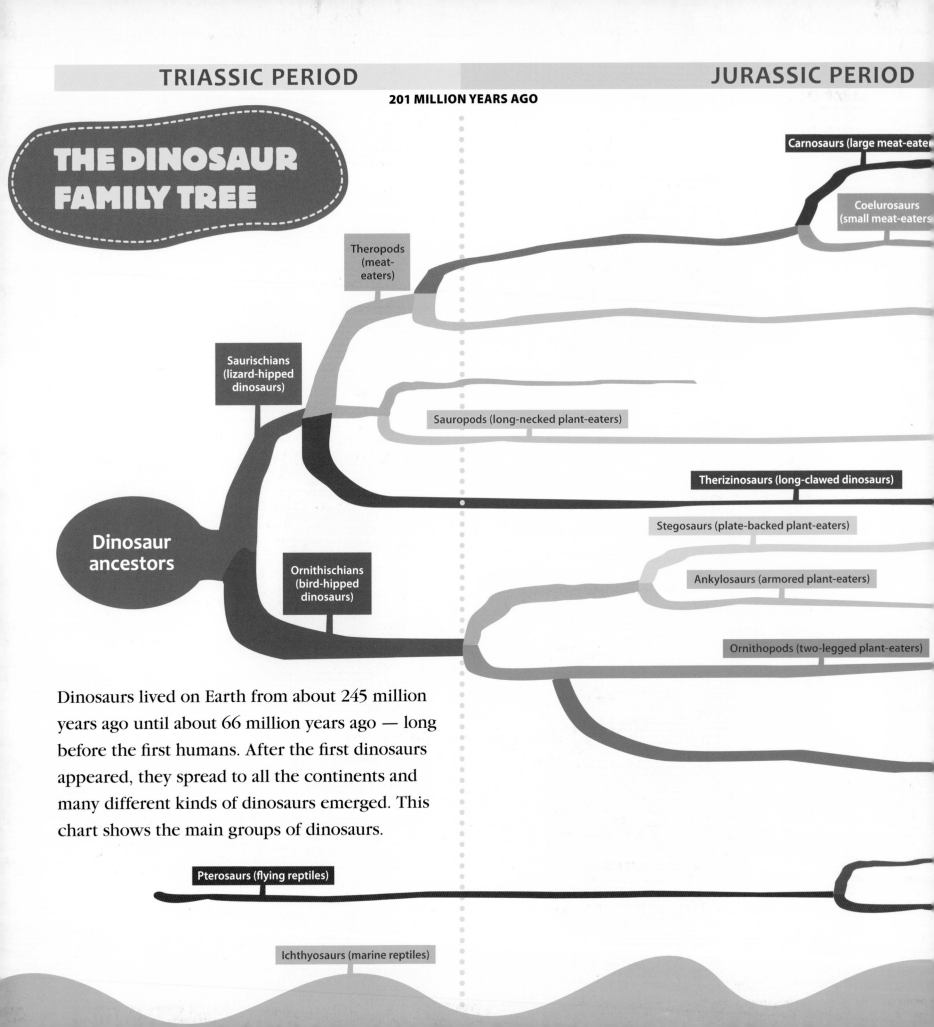

THE DINOSAUR FAMILY TREE

Carnosaurs (large meat-eaters)

Coelurosaurs (small meat-eaters)

Theropods (meat-eaters)

Saurischians (lizard-hipped dinosaurs)

Sauropods (long-necked plant-eaters)

Therizinosaurs (long-clawed dinosaurs)

Stegosaurs (plate-backed plant-eaters)

Dinosaur ancestors

Ankylosaurs (armored plant-eaters)

Ornithischians (bird-hipped dinosaurs)

Ornithopods (two-legged plant-eaters)

Dinosaurs lived on Earth from about 245 million years ago until about 66 million years ago — long before the first humans. After the first dinosaurs appeared, they spread to all the continents and many different kinds of dinosaurs emerged. This chart shows the main groups of dinosaurs.

Pterosaurs (flying reptiles)

Ichthyosaurs (marine reptiles)